BUGATTI CHIRON

W0006429

By K.C. Kelley

Kaleidoscope
Minneapolis, MN

BIGFOOT BOOKS

The Quest for Discovery Never Ends

This edition first published in 2021 by Kaleidoscope Publishing, Inc.

No part of this publication may be reproduced in whole or in part without written permission of the publisher.

For information regarding permission, write to Kaleidoscope Publishing, Inc. 6012 Blue Circle Drive Minnetonka, MN 55343

Library of Congress Control Number 2020936062

ISBN 978-1-64519-259-6 (library bound) 978-1-64519-327-2 (ebook)

Text copyright © 2021 by Kaleidoscope Publishing, Inc. All-Star Sports, Bigfoot Books, and associated logos are trademarks and/or registered trademarks of Kaleidoscope Publishing, Inc.

Printed in the United States of America.

FIND ME IF YOU CAN!

Bigfoot lurks within one of the images in this book. It's up to you to find him!

TABLE OF
CONTENTS

Chapter 1
Meet the Monster

How fast is the Bugatti Chiron? Imagine this: You're standing on a football field. You run to the far end and then halfway back. The world's fastest runner would take about 15 seconds to do that. You might need 30.

A Bugatti Chiron covers that distance in one second.

The Chiron's 16-cylinder engine can put out more than 1,500 horsepower.

150 yards. One . . . second. Wow!

Andy Wallace is one of the few people to know what that's like. The British racer tested the Bugatti Chiron 300 Sport. At a track in Germany, he strapped on his helmet and climbed in.

The Chiron engine turned over with a mighty roar. Wallace made sure the track was clear. He got the green light. He pushed down the gas pedal.

And his world turned to speed!

PARTS OF A
BUGATTI CHIRON

Tiny cargo space

LED headlights

Bugatti badge

Seven-speed
transmission

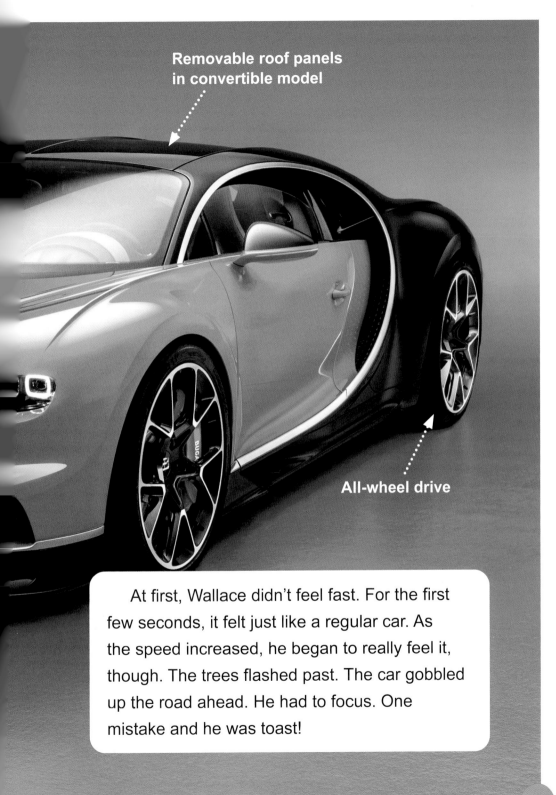

Removable roof panels in convertible model

All-wheel drive

At first, Wallace didn't feel fast. For the first few seconds, it felt just like a regular car. As the speed increased, he began to really feel it, though. The trees flashed past. The car gobbled up the road ahead. He had to focus. One mistake and he was toast!

Wallace was watching the road. He kept going faster and faster. He flew around curves! He hit the **straightaway** and poured it on. Would he make it? Would the car hold together?

Wallace kept his eyes focused ahead. If he had been watching the speed dial, he would have seen this: The dial read 305 miles per hour. A new record!

The Chiron is the fastest **production car** around. Bugatti is one of the world's most famous car brands. Together, they have set a new standard for supercars.

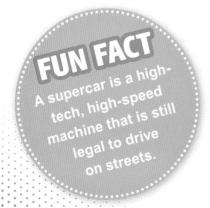

FUN FACT
A supercar is a high-tech, high-speed machine that is still legal to drive on streets.

What makes the Chiron so fast? It's the engine. Wallace had a 1,578-horsepower motor in gear. A superfast Lamborghini Aventador has a 770-horsepower engine. The Chiron is almost twice as powerful!

The average American car has less than 200 horses. The car Wallace was driving was more than seven times stronger than your car!

The Chiron engine has 16 **cylinders**. Most cars on the road today have just four. Cylinders move very fast and turn the car's **crankshaft**. That long car part turns the wheels. The more cylinders you have, the faster you can go.

A supercar like this needs a super body. The Chiron's design helps it move extra fast. The air flows over its skin like water.

Less weight also equals more speed. The Chiron's body is made of carbon fiber. This material is super-strong. Compared to metal, it is very light.

Going fast means no distractions. The Chiron doesn't have video info screens like many cars. There is no radio. There's not even much storage space. This is a car to drive fast—but not on the family trip!

Pick from several classy colors for your leather Chiron interior.

WHERE THE BUGATTI CHIRON IS MADE

Molsheim, France

Poland

Germany

France

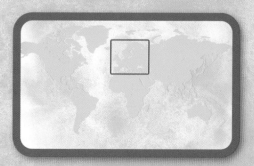

Chapter 2

Bugatti Beginnings

Ettore Bugatti came from an artistic family. His father was a famous furniture designer. His brother was a sculptor. Ettore combined art with his love of speed.

Famous Bugatti racing cars got their start before World War I. Some of the Bugatti racers are on display at car museums.

He first worked at a bicycle factory. He put a motor on a tricycle! In 1905, he designed his first race car for a German company. By 1909, he was running his own car company!

In 1911, a Bugatti car came in second at the French Grand Prix. Ettore was on his way to international fame!

More Bugatti racing cars followed. A 1924 car called the Type 35 won more than 500 races!

Still, Ettore wanted more. In 1926, he made the Royale. The factory only made six. It was the most expensive car in the world! Until he died in 1947, Ettore made beautiful car after beautiful car. Sadly, his company did not last long without him. It closed in 1956.

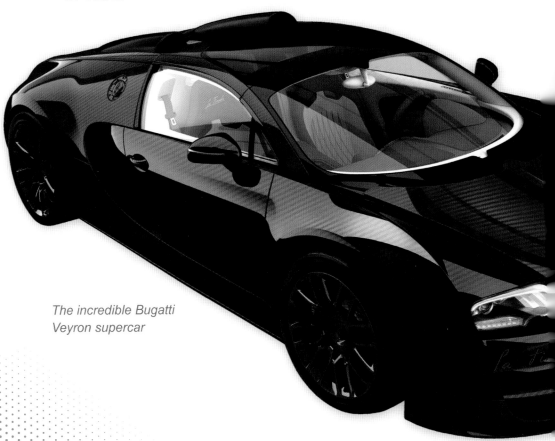

The incredible Bugatti Veyron supercar

A Bugatti Royale at a car museum

However, in 1998, Volkswagen brought back the Bugatti name. Amazing new cars started coming out. The Veyron debuted in 2005. It was 1,001 horsepower! It set a world record at 267 mph.

Soon, another Bugatti would break that record!

Chapter 3

A Rare Beast

Bugatti knew it could do more. Its designers and engineers went to work. In March 2016, the first Chiron was shown at the Geneva Auto Show.

People who saw it were amazed! It was bigger, more powerful, and faster than the Veyron.

From the start, the Chiron was something very special. "We are not talking about transportation," said Wolfgang Durheimer, head of Bugatti. "We are talking about being very fast, being very unusual, being top of the top."

How special? Bugatti only makes about 50 Chirons a year!

FUN FACT
The first Geneva Auto Show was in 1905, when Bugatti was just starting out.

THE
BUGATTI CHIRON
IN DETAIL

COST: $2.99 million (United States)

Height: 3 feet, 11.7 inches (1.2 m)

Width: 6 feet, 8 inches (2 meters)

LENGTH: 14 feet, 11 inches (4.5 m)

WEIGHT: 4,400 pounds (1,995 kg)

TOP SPEED: 261 miles per hour (420 kph)

TIME FROM 0-60 MPH: 2.3 seconds

The Chiron Andy Wallace drove hit 305 mph. The Chiron sold to the public can only go 261 mph. Why? The tires can't handle higher speeds! Wallace's car had special tires.

Titanium brakes stop the car. Any other metal would overheat! The headlights are high-powered LEDs. The headlight area also takes in air. That air flows to the brakes to cool them.

The Chiron Sport is made to be even fancier than the "regular" Chiron. More carbon fiber makes it stronger. A larger engine makes it faster. Its design helps it handle high speeds. The Sport can only be driven on a track.

Bugatti also made two new Chirons for 2020. Only 20 Chiron Sport 110 Ans were made. The name means "110 years." It honors the year Bugatti started

Car fans check out the beautiful 110 Ans Chiron in 2020.

his company. The 110 Ans is painted to show the French flag. Bugattis are made in France.

The Super Sport 300+ is your chance to drive like Andy Wallace. This special car is set up just like his. The 300+ owner can drive her car that fast—300-mph-plus!

Chapter 4

Super Speed!

Wallace kept his foot down. The miles sped by. The Chiron engine growled as it neared top speed. Wallace was going so fast, he had to watch out for wind. Even a tiny **gust** could push a fast car off track.

He hit 280 mph. That's when his driving skills really kicked in. "When you start to go past that, you have to be really, really careful," he said later.

The Chiron he was in cost more than $3 million. You bet he was *very* careful!

FUN FACT
You could buy 150 Toyota Corollas for the price of one Chiron!

Wallace began to slow down. He didn't want to. He wanted to stay out there all day! But the Chiron's tires were beginning to wear down. They could not put up with that much speed.

The British ace steered the Chiron into the **pit area**. As he climbed from the car, he had a huge grin on his face.

"What a car!" he said. "What a ride!"

Lucky Andy!

LEGO
CHIRON

Take one million Lego pieces—and a LOT of expert help—and you have the Lego Chiron! In 2018, Lego created this amazing car. They used "Technic" blocks. Only the tires were not Lego pieces. The electric motor was made from more than 2,000 special blocks. And the Lego Chiron drove! No, not 305 mph . . . but it does go 12 mph!

BEYOND
THE BOOK

After reading the book, it's time to think about what you learned. Try the following exercises to jumpstart your ideas.

RESEARCH

FIND OUT MORE. Where would you go to find out more about your favorite cars? Find out what company makes the car and locate its website. What information do the companies provide? What other sources of car information can you find?

CREATE

GET ARTISTIC. Cars start with creative artists and designers. Time for you to take a shot! Get art materials and create a great, new car. Will you make it a sports car? A sedan? A race car? What colors will you paint it? What features can you give it? Let your imagination go for a spin!

DISCOVER

DIG DEEPER. How can you make a car out of Lego or blocks or other materials? Check out the Bugatti Chiron. You probably don't have enough blocks to make that one, but build what you can! Can you make a Chiron? How about designing and building your own car? Try it!

GROW

GO TO A CAR SHOW. Car shows are a great way to see lots of cool cars up-close. Check your local events calendar, or ask at a car dealer for upcoming events. You can find shows of old cars and new cars, sports cars and classic cars. Go to a show and find a new favorite car to love!

RESEARCH NINJA

Visit *www.ninjaresearcher.com/2596* to learn how
to take your research skills and book report writing to the next level!

RESEARCH

DIGITAL
LITERACY
TOOLS

SEARCH LIKE A PRO
Learn about how to use search engines to find useful websites.

FACT OR FAKE?
Discover how you can tell a trusted website from an untrustworthy resource.

TEXT DETECTIVE
Explore how to zero in on the information you need most.

SHOW YOUR WORK
Research responsibly— learn how to cite sources.

WRITE

GET TO THE POINT
Learn how to express your main ideas.

PLAN OF ATTACK
Learn prewriting exercises and create an outline.

DOWNLOADABLE
REPORT
FORMS

Further Resources

BOOKS

Garstecki, Julia, and Stephanie Derkovitz. *Bugatti Chiron (Epic Cars).* North Mankato, MN: Black Rabbit Books, 2019.

Oachs, Emily Rose. *Bugatti Chiron (Car Crazy).* Mankato, MN: Bellwether Media, 2018.

Singh, Asavari. *How to Draw the Fastest, Coolest Cars.* Minneapolis, MN: Capstone, 2015.

WEBSITES

FACTSURFER

Factsurfer.com gives you a safe, fun way to find more information.

1. Go to www.factsurfer.com.

2. Enter "Bugatti Chiron" into the search box and click 🔍

3. Select your book cover to see a list of related websites.

Glossary

auction: an event in which bids are taken to buy things.

crankshaft: a long, tubular car part that leads from the engine to the wheels.

cylinders: tubes; in a car, cylinders move up and down to turn the crankshaft.

gust: a short burst of wind.

horsepower: a measurement of the power of an engine or a motor.

pit area: places near a race track where cars are worked on.

production car: a car made for use on the street.

straightaway: a long part of a race track without any curves.

Index

PHOTO CREDITS

About the Author

K.C. Kelley has written more than 100 books for young readers on a wide variety of topics. His subjects include sports of all kinds, space, animals, science, history, and biography. Thanks to Conor Buckley for research assistance on this book.